AF584695

Dear Teen Self

For information contact: www.dearteenself.com

Book Cover design by Nia E. designs

Illustrations by Raheem Dade

Photography by Floyd Shade

ISBN: 978-0-692-57544-4

First Edition: November 2015

This book is dedicated to the teen girl that is ready to give up because the pain is too real. Do not give up and know you will make it through your storm.

Acknowledgments

I want to take this time to acknowledge people that have been paramount in the success of this book. I want to begin by stating the birth of this book came from a place of confusion, yet, I am thankful for it. There is always a rainbow after a storm, so I am thankful for my storm. I want to start by thanking my friends and family for their never-ending support. Thanks to my mom for helping with the production of the book and simply always being mom. Brittany and Adam, you two caught the bulk of my worry, frustration, doubt, fear and more the most throughout this journey. I am forever indebted to you both for your patience, care and guidance. My graphic designer, Taniah English and illustrator, Raheem Dade, probably wanted to give up on me. However, I am so glad you didn't. I am so thankful for your patience with me being a newbie to design. Thank you to my editor Stephanie Coalson. You were so kind while handling me, my manuscript, and hyperactivity.

I want to thank all of the teenagers that I have met during this journey. Every single one of you meant something to me and to this purpose. You all kept me going, kept me in the moment and understanding why finishing this book was so important. Whenever I shared I was writing a book for teens, you encouraged me to finish stating it was needed. I am truly doing this for you all. Last but not least, I want to thank all the non-profit leaders in the Philadelphia area. Since I am not from Philadelphia, so many of you have embraced me, introduced me to your networks and trusted me to meet the youth you work with. You believed in me and my vision enough to allow me in your lives. For that, I am beyond appreciative.

"My life was not my own until I took control."

~Jaynay C.

INSERT SELFIE

Introduction

I am overwhelmed with joy as I am writing this because it means I have completed my first book. This book should be used as a tool to help you get through some of the challenges that you may be experiencing. My teen years were hell and I am grateful to be here to discuss those years. I am a 28-year-old Marriage and Family therapist living in her purpose. This was my dream, now a reality. I want you to know all your dreams can be a reality. Life may start off rocky, but you have the chance to change that. This book is also intended to be your diary. I want you to write in it as you read. I do not want you to miss the messages or feelings as you identify with a scenario.

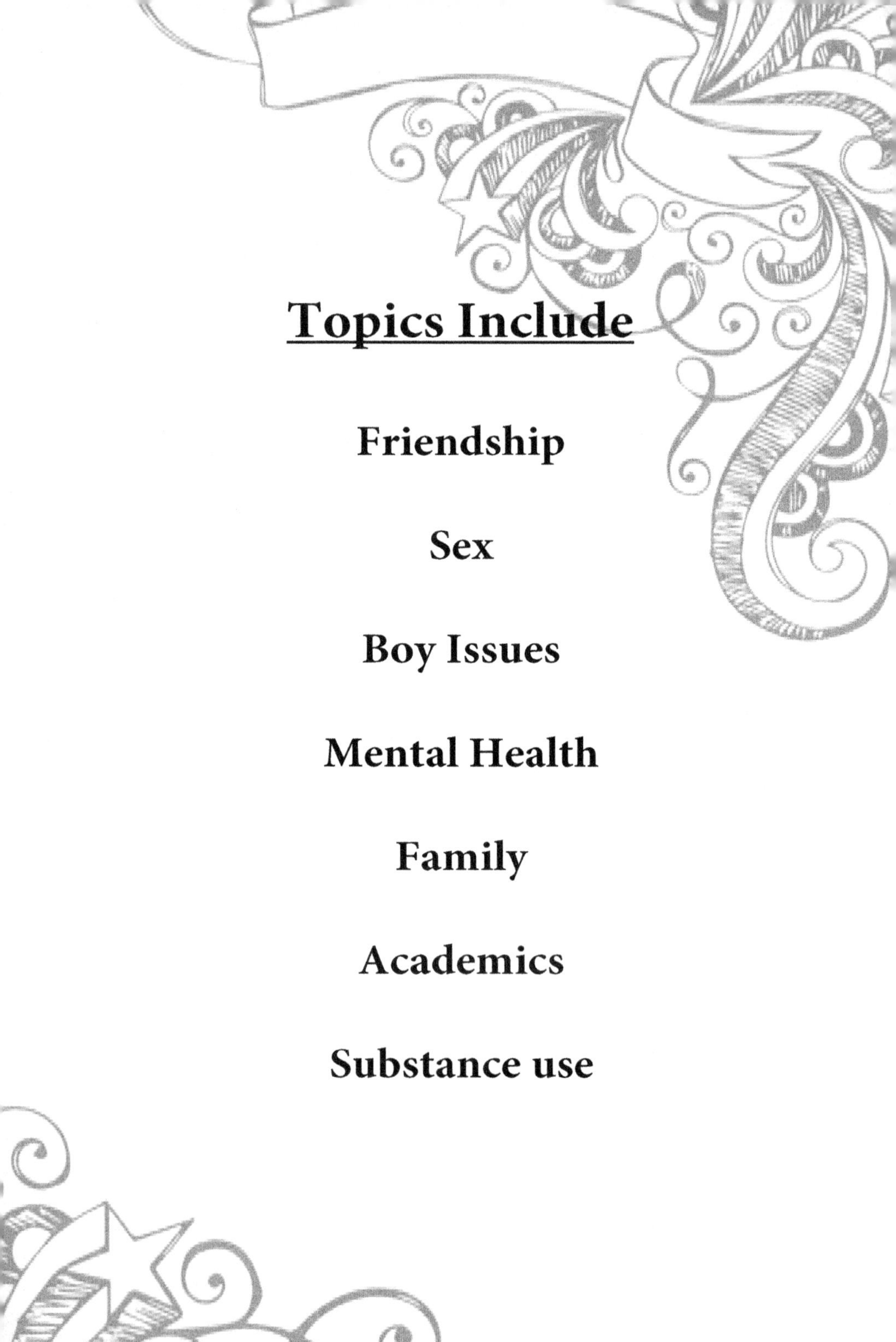

Topics Include

Friendship

Sex

Boy Issues

Mental Health

Family

Academics

Substance use

DTS Pledge

{Recite and sign}

Dear Teen Self,

I love you! You are unique and beautiful in many ways. You never have to apologize for being yourself. You do need to choose to heal on purpose and make positive choices. I am in control of my happiness. Girl, you are amazing and you will make it.

Love,

____

Signature

dear teen self

There's nothing wrong with not being popular

High school was an absolute pain in my BLEEP. The girls hated me because all the guys liked me. (That was not my problem) However, it was a reality that was obnoxious. I experienced this issue in high school and in middle Okay, I may be exaggerating but it felt like the entire school. Wait, it really was the entire school. I never decided to be popular, it just happened. Popularity is not always gold, although it sparkles. Do not strive for popularity. More importantly, do not do things to make yourself become popular.

I cared if people like me

Hmm. So, I definitely told myself all through middle & high school that I didn't care if people liked me: that was a lie.

I absolutely cared about if people liked me because I am HUMAN. It is fine if your feelings are hurt because people don't like you. Just don't let it consume you. Being consumed could look like saying "Fxxk the world" or "crying every night." Acknowledge you are hurt, realize not everyone is going to like you, and understand that is alright.

Someone not liking you does not mean you aren't valuable. Do not change to fit in.

I did want my dad to be around

I did not realize how much I actually wanted my father to be in my life. I thought he didn't affect my life for a long time, but the truth is that he did. Your father should be the first man to teach you how another man should treat you. He should also be the first man to tell you that you are beautiful. Let me be honest about my experience with my father. I know my father and he was technically around. That means I knew how to reach him. I spent some summers with him growing up and I also remember the times I haven't heard from him in years. He missed so many birthdays that it wasn't a surprise when he asked me one day, when was my birthday. The moral of this story is, understand that you need that male role model and openly express how it makes you feel.

Write some thoughts below about your experience with your father. Do you think it has affected you?

My life depends on me

I always blamed everyone else for the poor choices I made. Yes, my teen years were tough, but I made them tougher with my decisions. Deciding to cut school because I was depressed and distraught over what was happening in my life did not make my life better. My life depended on me and it still does. Consider the choices you are making and ask if they will help or hurt you long term.

ARE YOU MAKING **GOOD** OR **POOR** CHOICES FOR YOUR LIFE?

Circle good or poor

People will think what they want

People will think what they want about you. Let them. Whether you do good or bad, just DO YOU! I struggled so much trying to understand why other people thought the way they did about me and it really was not helpful. You know why? Because I cannot read minds or change for every person I encounter that doesn't like my hair or outfit choice.

Stop trying to be a grown-up

I was a grown teenager. Dating all the older boys and engaging in some risky behavior. I am grateful that I was not caught up in a situation that would alter my life drastically. However, I cannot say that will be your fate. Slow down and enjoy your time as a teenager.

Ask yourself why you are engaging in risky behaviors. Jot your responses below. Remember to be honest with yourself.

Your body is magical

Your body is a temple. Cliché right? Oh well, it is still accurate. As ladies, our bodies control a lot of things and we need to handle them with care. I now think of sexual interactions as deposits and spiritual withdrawals. If the person has negative energy, they will deposit that energy into you and take some of your good energy. *Protect your body.*

Strive for greatness right now

Listen, you are royalty and you need to believe that. There's no need to wait until you are older to strive for greatness.

DO IT NOW

INTERESTS	*HOBBIES*

Don't limit yourself

Believe in yourself and that the sky is truly the limit. I'm writing this book after telling myself I wanted to be an author since high school. Yes, it took me a while, but I did it.

Create your own lane

Don't fit in? Good!! Create your own lane. You have freedom to be creative and create your own safe place. I never felt like I fit in or that I was understood. It wasn't until recently I began to feel comfortable with myself and created my own path. During this reflection, I also realized I was battling this since I was a young girl.

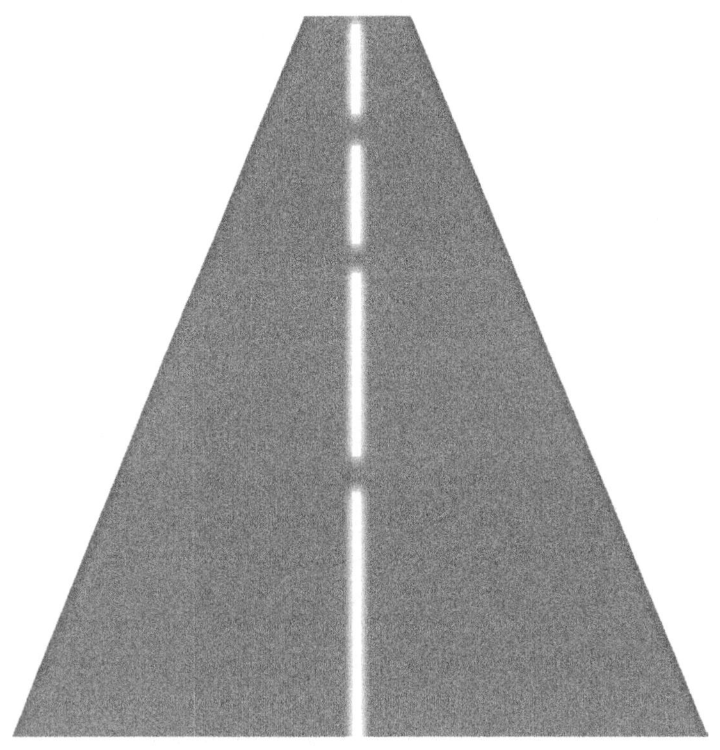

Something is wrong if you don't have friends of the same sex

So, don't roll your eyes, because this is the truth. Do you know how many times I've said and heard girls say, "I don't hang out with girls. They're catty and can't be trusted." This is so backwards. You are pretty much saying *YOU* are catty and can't be trusted. Think about it. You are included in the category of girl, so what makes you different? Absolutely nothing!

If you cannot maintain friends of the same sex, you are probably insecure, petty and cannot be trusted. We often put expectations, sometimes unrealistic, on our friends based on past situations and fear. You have to be open to new friends without prejudging.

Don't feel guilty for being the pretty girl

This may seem shallow, but I was considered a pretty girl in school that had the popular boyfriends. Since no one liked me, I gave people a reason to not like me. Now that I look back on that experience, I needed to be comfortable with my body and looks. If I was, I wouldn't have stooped to those girls' level in the first place. Be your beautiful self, girl! They'll get over it and if they don't, that's their choice.

OMG everyone likes me, aside from the haters

Everyone likes you at school? GREAT!! Do not let naysayers change your personality. Only you will suffer in the end. This may seem like a contradiction to another tip where I talk about everyone hating me. I should have been clear and said the girls hated me. Here is the true reason why, I was likable. I have a great personality and everyone cannot say the same. Teachers loved me, coaches loved me and, of course, the boys loved me. I was honestly a good person. I allowed those girls to interfere with my joy and that should have never happened.

Be the geek

If you are intellectual, go ahead and be that. I was one of the salutatorian's in middle school and began high school with all honors. Ask me about the rest of high school, LOL. I bombed my sophomore year and I felt like an idiot. I allowed my emotional state to overshadow what I was good at, which was my academics. I went from a 3.67 GPA with all honors classes to a 0.86.

WTH, right?!

If you are a nerd or geek, get comfortable and be yourself no matter what. If you are going through emotional issues, focusing on your education is a positive coping skill, unlike what I did.

Don't lose your imagination

As children, we have a vivid imagination that we often lose as we grow older. We are repeatedly told it is time to grow up and put away our childish ways. Do not fall for that. You need your imagination to survive in the world. Your creativity and ability to be innovative will set you apart from everyone else. Not to mention it will help you cope with life's stressors.

Imagine your safe place or your dream life.

Learn to trust yourself

Trust is such a touchy topic, right? Well let me start by saying, you have to trust yourself first in order to trust anyone else. Trusting yourself is one difficult task. I did not know how to trust myself as a teenager. I made poor decisions and I often thought I was not going to make it to adulthood.

Let's process why that is. I did not think I deserved better so I purposely chose the destructive path. I lost ALL trust in adults and life. I no longer believed in so called positivity or negativity. I was literally numb. I believed my pain came from everything that was not supposed to be painful like family or school. So through my experiences, I learned even the safest places breed pain. My advice to you is to trust yourself and your worth, even when those that are meant to protect you fall short.

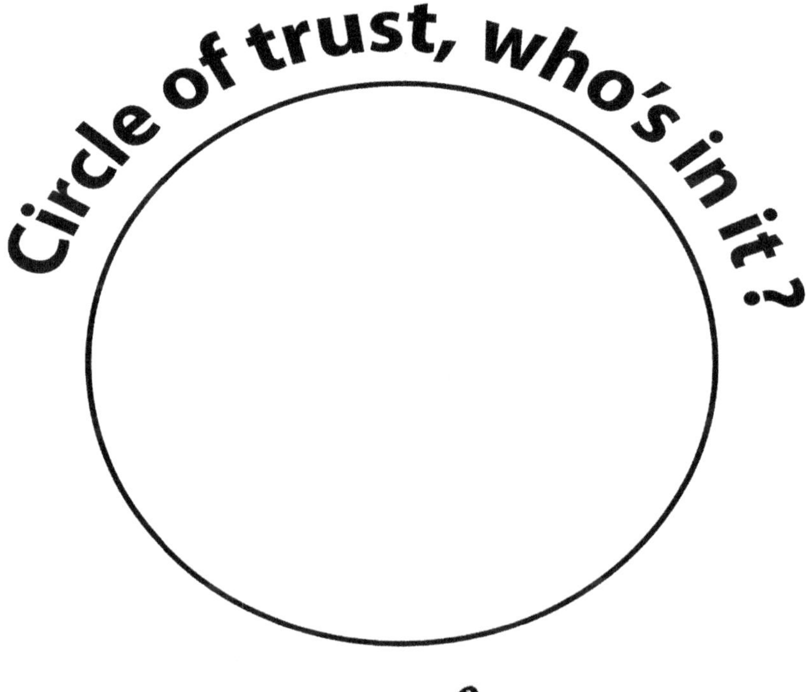

Talk to your parents

If you are lucky enough to have your parents in your life, talk to them. I have a secret for you. Come closer…a little closer… they actually want the best for you and they are trying to protect you. Crazy, right? They can be annoying; I get it. But think about why they're so annoying. Could it be that they are trying to keep you from doing something that could be harmful?Here's another secret: they probably went through a similar experience and made it through. Therefore, what they have to say may not be so bad or irrelevant.

Ask questions

As a teenager, I did NOT know everything. I often questioned life in general. So many of my thoughts went unnoticed because I kept them in the abyss of my mind. If you have questions, don't be afraid to ASK. Getting that question answered could save you. I am aware you may not want to talk to your parents. That is why it is important to find an adult you can confide in.

Write 4 questions that you have on your mind.

1.

2.

3.

4.

Your attitude is a reflection of you

If you ask anyone I went to high school with, they will tell you I had a nasty attitude. If looks could kill everyone would be dead. I definitely came across as evil. I was not an evil person, though; I was hurting inside and I did not know how to properly express it. Couple that with everyone hating me because I had two of the most popular boys as my boyfriends (at separate times, of course).

Do you like what you see?

Be the person you hope everyone else is

If you wish people were more compassionate, **BE** more compassionate. If you wish people were more understanding, **BE** more understanding. If you wish people were forgiving, **BE** more forgiving yourself. Get my drift? What is the point of complaining about people not being a certain way and then you turn around and act like them?

"IF WE LOSE LOVE & RESPECT FOR EACH OTHER, THIS IS HOW WE FINALLY DIE."

~ MAYA ANGELOU

Check in Page

Still here with me? Jot down some thoughts and/or feelings here.

.... okay, let's get back to it.

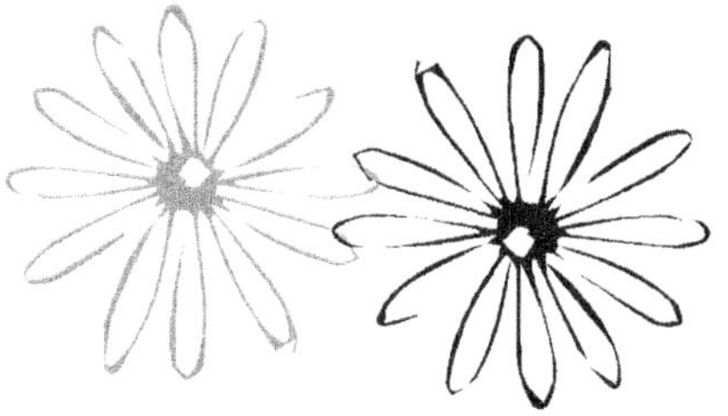

Your childhood isn't your future

Whew, I am not a preacher so I am not going to preach. However, you need to know that your childhood is not your future. The trials and tribulations won't last forever. I want you to repeat it **3** times. Matter of fact, I'll do it with you, let's go.

Your childhood is not your future

Your childhood is not your future

Your childhood is not your future

Guard your mind

Your mind may be the only thing keeping you sane in an environment that is negative so guard it at all costs. Do not let go of your dreams and hopes. Trust me; they will get you through the storm.

Use your passion to get through tough times

I had to hold on to my dreams of going to Spelman in order to make it through my hard experiences. I had to remember that I wanted to be a doctor and ultimately help teens like me from going down the path I was on. Believe the adults when they tell you that the path you're on is dangerous. It may be tough to navigate through it.

Use the maze exercise to navigate from where you are to your dreams. Label the lines to identify stressors and traumas you have endured.

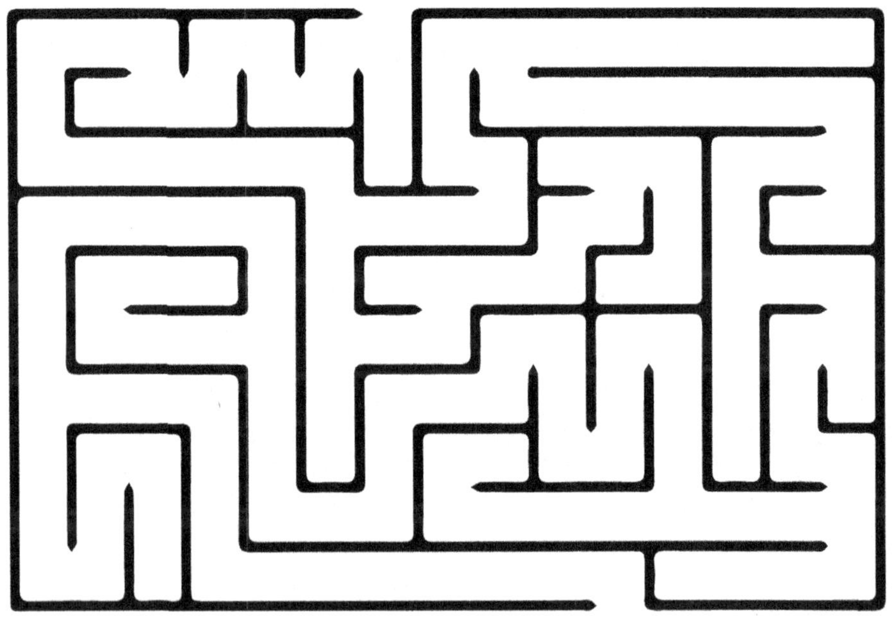

Cherish your ideas

If you are a dreamer, continue to be one and do not let people steal your shine. Miserable people do not want you to succeed. Cherish your ideas. While growing up, I held on to the idea that I would attend Spelman College after reading about them in an *Ebony* magazine. Once I began struggling, the thought of college made me get it together. I knew I wanted to be successful, turn my life around, and guess what? I did!!! I did not go to Spelman, but I did go to a Historically Black College or University (HBCU) and regained my confidence.

IDEA CLOUDS

(put your ideas in the clouds)

If most people are going left, go right

You do not always need to follow your peers. This is especially true if your self-esteem is low; because you might do anything to fit in. I smoked "weed" and drank every chance I got. I would leave school to go get high and drink 40 ounce beers. This behavior caused me to fail me many classes, lose interest in activities and put a strain on valuable relationships. Not to mention, I was exposed to environmental dangers while being under the influence.

What trends do you find yourself following?

Fill in the arrows.

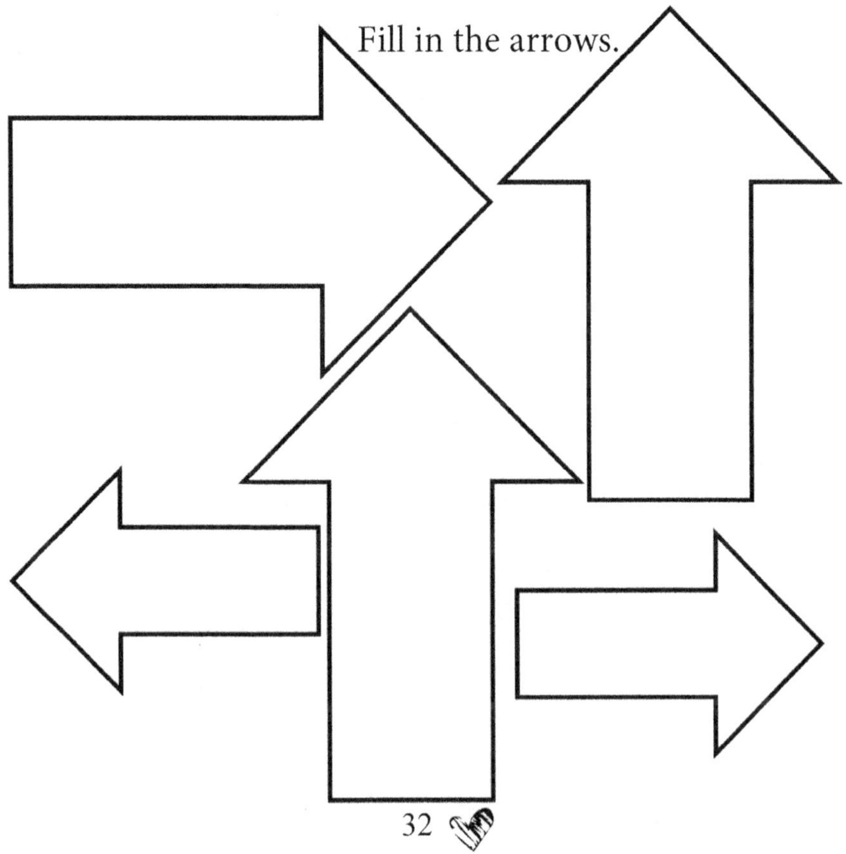

Be a better you, friend, sister, etc.

I was so mean as a teenager. I did not have a filter and I did not care how mad I made anyone. I thought it was their problem. However, as an adult I've realized how dumb that was. You have to be better if everything around you is falling apart. My situation was bad and I made it worse by being mean to people around me. I was an only child so I did not have those sibling experiences. If you do, be a better sibling. They are organic friends and we need all the love and support we can get.

Sister, Sister

I'm your keeper,

Friend o' friend,

No bond is deeper,

Self to self,

Don't forget to love you in the mirror.

~Jaynay C.

Not everyone is a hater

Our generation struggles with constructive criticism. Not everything you do is cool or cute and when someone tells you so, it doesn't make them a hater. You have no idea if people are trying to look out for you and they are telling you things that you need to hear.

A hater is defined as:

A person that simply cannot be happy for another person's success. So rather than be happy they make a point of exposing a perceived flaw in that person.

If you're doing something less-than-smart (stupid) like holding drugs for "bae," I'm not a hater for telling you it's dumb.

Encourage your friends

When you are a teen, your peers are the most important social group. Be a positive influence for your friends. There are enough negative influences. Choose to be a leader.

Honor your parents

I had an extremely rocky relationship with my parents. I'm not sure which relationship was rockier or for what reason. It could be my mother because I lived with her or it could be my father because he was in and out of my life. Either way I needed to honor them. Although I did not like how certain things were handled, honoring them was for my own benefit, not theirs. I want you to understand that no matter what people do; you have control over how to respond to it.

I was extremely disrespectful to my parents and I thought that I was justified because of how I perceived my struggles. Then I realized that I was still miserable because I was purposefully being mean. That should never be OK. No matter what I thought, they gave me life and now I have the choice to live it positively.

You are somebody

I struggled with my identity and not thinking I had much to offer the world. I often felt I was ugly and that I would not amount to anything. Since I felt that way, I made choices that reflected those negative inner beliefs. I am here to tell you that you are somebody and that you deserve more. Do not destroy your youth.

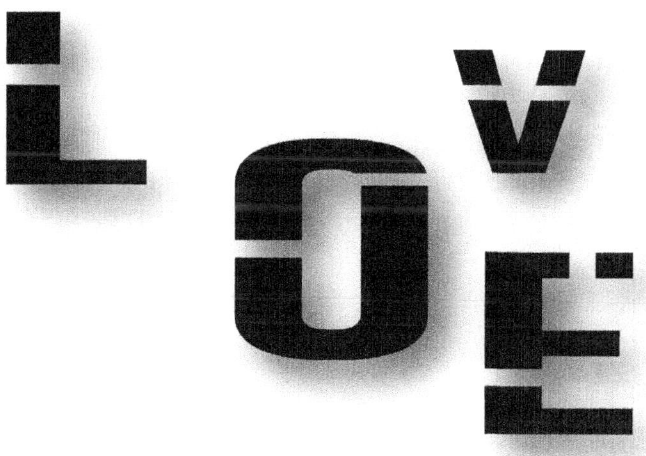

Love comes in variations

Seeking love if you come from a broken home can be good; however, it can go bad easily. The most common way girls go looking for love is from a man. That man is usually older and preying on your vulnerability. I have been there.

I dated the school-aged boys, the older boys and the boys in different cities, all to find love. Each situation was different and loaded with multiple problems. Some were age appropriate while the age gap in other situations were simply CRAZY.

It is important to love yourself in order to focus your energy correctly. Loving yourself is the only way others can know how to love you. In the meantime, find love in a hobby. It is a more productive way to manage your emotions then lying under a boy or man.

All attention isn't good attention

All attention is not good attention. I had a boyfriend in high school who offered me a lot of attention. Initially, I loved it, however, over time, I realized how toxic the attention was. He was controlling and verbally abusive. Of course, it did not start like that, but it certainly ended that way. He was broken and I was broken which is not healthy. Two broken pieces don't make a whole. I'm thankful I made it out of the situation with my sanity. Believe me when I say all love isn't good love and it starts within.

Don't think a boy is going to solve your problems

Appreciate it for what it is, not make it what it is not. If you choose to have sex, that is your choice. However, understand what you are or aren't getting into. Do not place other expectations on him without there being a discussion. You will get your feelings hurt and they are already fragile.

Do not fall victim to the baby talk

Don't be the girl that thinks having a baby is going to change your world and everything will be fine. If you think having a baby will make you feel more loved or will reduce the negative factors in your life…think again and again!

Babies require constant care, attention, and nurturing, which you still require from your parents as a teen.

Do you even know what love and care actually look like?

Yeah, I didn't think so. Let me know if you no longer want to go out to parties so you can stay at home feeding your baby and changing diapers.

•Black and Hispanic women have the highest teen pregnancy rates (100 and 84 per 1,000 women aged 15–19, respectively); whites have the lowest rate (38% per 1,000).

Be your own savior

I was hoping someone came to save me. I asked God over and over again to save me. I often thought, "Come on, God. Get to pushing." Then, I realized there was still something in my control, so I controlled it, in a positive manner. Teens, control what you can. If that means you can do hair and that will get you out of the house, then go do that. Be a good student, go to class. That's in your control. If you can act, go act. Do what's in your control because all you're going to do if you're truly frustrated, is frustrate yourself more.

Decide what you want for yourself

You need to claim your own life and declare what you want for yourself. If you want to be a loser, then guess what? You'll be a loser. If you want to be successful, you will be successful. You have to make up your mind about WHO you want to be. I knew I didn't want to be a woman with three kids with different fathers not understanding what went wrong. Take control now and decide what you want for yourself

Just be a teenager

Don't try to grow up too fast. It's not necessary. Be a teenager or I'll give you one of my bills to pay, LOL.

Find someone to talk to

Find someone that is going to be a confidant for you. This person will allow you to express your deepest feelings and concerns. Even if you don't talk to them every day, just have a person to go to. There was a time when I didn't have anyone and wished I did. Then, I was fortunate enough to have my cheerleading coach and my class advisor to stick it out with me. They helped me get where I needed to go and helped me focus and maintain my energy. I knew if I was in a emotional crisis emotionally, they would be there.

Forgive yourself

You are going to make mistakes because you do not know all the answers. For some teens guidance is given, for others guidance isn't available, so that will make a difference. Forgive yourself, regardless, because we all make poor choices.

Nothing can be undone in life. Whatever mistake is made; you can still thrive. Learn the lesson from your mistake and move on.

"Forgiveness is for you and no one else."

~ Jaynay C.

Check in Page

How are you feeling so far?

Let off some steam here……

……. okay, let's get back to it.

Sex is not just pleasure

Sex is more than fun, it's dangerous. When you think about all the diseases and infections that are out here, you should second guess who you sleep with. Understand the function of your body, see a doctor regularly and know the risks involved with having sex.

Here's a few statistics for you:

* Although 15- to 24-year-olds represent only one-quarter of the sexually active population, they account for nearly half (9.1 million) of the 18.9 million new cases of STDs each year.

* Trichomoniasis and chlamydia are the next most common STD diagnoses among 15- to 24-year-olds. Combined, they account for slightly more than one-third of all diagnoses each year. Genital herpes and gonorrhea together account for about 12% of diagnoses. HIV, syphilis, and hepatitis B account for less than 1% of diagnoses.

Use protection

Hey, you. Yes, you. YOU can get HIV or Herpes. They really don't have a type and don't care if you have straight A's or not. They also don't care about birth control and they don't care if it's your first time.

- Young people aged 13–24 accounted for about 21% of all new HIV diagnoses in the United States in 2011.

Be responsible beyond condoms

Young ladies, you also need to take birth control. If you want to do adult things, do adult things. You really do not want to figure out how to make an appointment at Planned Parenthood and sit in utter fear as you pee on a stick or get a blood test to determine if you're pregnant. I have been there and my life flashed before my eyes. I even realized that the dude who could have been the father was not someone I wanted to be in my life forever.

Every time you are about to have sex, ask yourself if you are willing to have him in your life FOREVER & more.

Don't have sex

If you're already broken, sex will confuse you. If you do have sex, always use protection. Since I may be over zealous with this tip, I want you to understand the value sex has for you. So ask yourself these 5 questions.

1. Am I having sex for myself?

2. Do I think it adds value to my life?

3. Am I doing it to fit in?

4. Am I being pressured?

5. Do I know everything about sex?

Don't go on video

As a clinician, I have had to deal with so many young girls being depressed and having multiple suicide attempts due to being ridiculed after being on tape for the boy they loved. It is all right to like/love him, but be smart and never be recorded. If it doesn't feel right, it isn't right and you need to remove yourself from the situation. Loyalty at this phase is not necessary.

Don't send nude pics

Let's list all the positive reasons you should do this...

(Crickets chirping)
There is no good reason to send your naked body to someone.

Here are some reasons why you should not send pics in case you couldn't think of any:

1. It could be used against you if that person gets upset
2. It can be circulated via text and possibly the internet
3. You could be criminally charged because it's technically child pornography you are transmitting

I have worked with numerous teens who were blackmailed with their pictures/videos and were ridiculed in school. This was so daunting that they tried committing suicide. **This is not a joke.** I should also mention that once it's on the internet, you cannot get it off.

He doesn't love you, well,not like that

Now, hear me out on this one. I do believe in teenage love, but it's infatuation more than anything. You are infatuated with each other and you should enjoy that. Just don't risk your safety or your life for infatuation.

Choose your partners carefully

Having sex requires a lot of responsibility and you need to respect yourself enough to choose a worthy guy. Not the street dude that calls you out your name as you walk by. That is SO not cute. Your choice in a man is a reflection of you. Be mindful of whom you share your spirit and body with.

Have fun appropriately

I found myself in very sketchy situations wondering what was about to happen to me. I often wondered why I was even in those situations to begin with. Many situations were completely my fault for skipping school. There were a few close calls and a lot of them dealt with sex. Sex that I didn't want to have but would have consented to because I thought I led him on just by being in his house during school hours.

You should not have a clue about baby mama drama

I dated a guy who put his "baby-mom" in a headlock because she was trying to attack me. There is no reason why you should ever have to deal with that. You are growing up faster than is necessary if you can relate. I should also note that dating a man with children as a teenager is completely out of your league.

Understand the signs of an abusive relationship

I was in an abusive relationship and I had no idea until I went to college. I was in a domestic violence workshop for the psychology club when the signs penetrated my mind.
As the woman spoke, my mind naturally went back to that one relationship and at that moment I realized I was in an abusive relationship and never knew. Once I knew, I needed to heal from it because I was operating as if I was still in that abusive situation.

Warning Signs

Controlling behavior

Blaming you for their behavior

Hitting you

Name calling

Stopping you from hanging with friends

Everyone doesn't have to like you, but you don't have to give them a reason

Not everyone will like you and that is fine. However, do not make it your business to give them a reason not to like you like my spiteful-self did. I thought, "Oh, you don't like me? Let me give you a reason then." This was unnecessary because I made myself look foolish when all I wanted was for people to like me.

Value your friendships (don't be shady)

I was shady, especially in middle school. Because I have experience, I'm writing this book. I valued my boyfriends more than my friendships because the boys showed me more interest. Girls didn't like me much. Understand that boys will always show more interest but that does not mean you have to give them your energy. Be sure that you have a life outside of your relationships with boys. I betrayed many friends for the sake of boys and I did not care. Friends were disposable in my mind.

Understand your moods

Sadness is sometimes more than just plain sadness. Be aware of your feelings and how long you have been feeling that way. It is quite normal to be sad and wanting to be alone, especially as a teenager. I thought endlessly about escaping the pain and I did escape in various ways. I harmed myself by smoking and not making safe choices. Self-harm/destruction comes in many forms. I was depressed as a teenager; however, I didn't know what that meant while growing up. I knew I was sad for months and lost interest in most of life. Mental health is important and real.

What do you know about mental health and how do you define it?

* Feelings of hopelessness can lead to feelings of suicide. If you are feeling suicidal talk to someone you know or call the national suicide prevention hotline.

1 (800) 273-8255

Know community resources

You need to know where to go to get help. I've been talking about my experiences, but I am aware some of your experiences may be worse than mine were. Locate the nearest police station; locate the nearest non-profit; locate the nearest shelter; and know numbers to call to get assistance. It's one thing to be sad and weary, but it's another thing to be lost and weary and have nowhere to turn.

Here are some Google search terms to use

Teen help

Non-profits in my area for teens

Teen programs

Teen depression

Teen Shelters

Teen Mental health

Remember to include your location as you search for resources

Manipulate the system

Let's face it. Some of you may be in a tough situation. But try to make it work for you. You are not the first and you won't be the last to go through struggles. Take advantage of people wanting to help and see it as a building block for your future.

Dress for your body type

If you have a huge bust, please wear the right size bra and the right size shirt. I was the girl with the big boobs since I was 12 and I HATED it. I often didn't dress myself appropriately because I was trying to act like I didn't have boobs in the first place. Dress for you and what you are comfortable in. DO not attempt to dress like everyone else if it comprises who you are.

Respect yourself

The value of this word no longer seems to exist. Respecting yourself means knowing your values and morals and not budging on them because of what others say to you. You need to know what you stand for or you will definitely fall for anything. Respecting yourself is how you present to the world your value.

Become a mentor

Find a greater purpose for your life. That may come in the form of being a mentor. Help someone else along his or her journey and see where that takes you. I always tried to remember that someone had it worse than me and that I shouldn't complain.

<u>Life is what you make it</u>

In life, we all have choices and you are in control of those choices. Just for clarity, not making a choice is still a choice. When everything around you is negative, you have the choice to be positive. It may not be easy, but you have a choice. Use it wisely. Jhene Aiko's song, W.A.Y.S is one of my favorite songs because it reminds me how difficult life can be and that I cannot give up.

… Life can get wild when, you're caught in the whirl wind
Lost in the whirl wind, you're chasing the wind

...That's why I keep going, I gotta keep going
I gotta keep going, I gotta keep going
I gotta show them, that I can keep going
I gotta keep going, I gotta keep going

~Jhene Aiko W.A.Y.S

Don't forget to kiss the frog

Just because a guy is popular and all the girls like him, doesn't mean he is the guy for you. Do not forget to talk to the guy who isn't super popular or not popular at all. You want to learn early that a man should treat you nicely and be respectful versus just being the cutest boy in school.

Date boys your age

Experiences are meant to be shared, however, certain things you do not need to experience until you're older. I dated people older than me all the time and thought it was super cute until I saw my older dude put his "baby mama" in a headlock because she tried to attack me. Of course, I could have thought that was endearing but it was actually scary. At that exact moment, I knew I was not ready for that type of situation.

<u>Check in Page</u>

Don't leave me; I have a few more things to share with you.

.... okay, let's get back to it.

Guard your sanity

My family drove me crazy–literally and figuratively. I would take long walks, smoke cigarettes, black & milds or weed in order to clear my mind. Walking the streets of Newark, NJ as a 15-year-old girl was not the smartest thing to do. Safety was not my concern. I am grateful I was never hurt during my wandering phase. However, that was better than what my mind went through in my home. That was my attempt to guard my sanity. I figured getting fresh air and walking would help calm me down. More importantly, I got out of the house causing me to question my sanity in the first place. These were my coping skills kicking in.

Invest in yourself and your dream

Dr. Martin Luther King, Jr. said it best when he gave his "I Have a Dream" speech and I know you have one, too. Invest in it!! Do not think you aren't good enough to achieve your dream because you are. You are worthy. Start to believe that now and your choices will change.

I am the **master of my life.**

I am **capable of success.**

I am **intelligent.**

I am **powerful.**

I am **worth it.**

Use "I" Statements

This may be all of my years of post-secondary education talking, but express yourself from your perspective. Your feelings are valid and you need to express them. It is easy to hide behind your pain instead of addressing it. Stating “I” gives you the power to take control of your feelings. The power of positive “I” statements can change your mood and how you view life. Recite the I statements above for motivation.

Don't play the blame game

The blame game tore me down as a teenager because it was everyone's fault but my own. Sure home was rough, but I chose to cut school and in turn, I failed most of my honors classes. I chose to cut school and escape. I just didn't know how to deal with my peers in my emotional state. Most days I looked bad and I didn't want anyone to see me. Even with all that, I still made the choices and I needed to be accountable for my choices. Once I stopped blaming others, I regained my power.

You'll bounce back

At every hurdle, I thought my life was over. You are resilient and strong. So get on up and keep strolling through life. I thought my life was over when I began failing sophomore year. I thought it was over when I had to go live with my father. I thought it was over when my boyfriend took another girl to prom. No matter what you think about it being over, just know it isn't over until you give up.

Be all that you can be right now

Are you waiting for something amazing to happen? Be the best *YOU* right *NOW*. I held back so much of my personality and I wish I hadn't. I grew up with insecurities that I didn't need to have and I wish I had realized my greatness earlier because it was always there. You do not always need approval and validation from others. Some, well, most people won't see your vision anyway.

JUST DO YOU

Volunteer in the community

If you think your situation is bad, go out in the community and help others. You might learn your situation isn't as bad as some others. On the other hand, you may realize it is as bad and you can find a friend and each of you can uplift the other. This also provides space to get out of your home while doing something positive.

Websites

www.Volunteennation.com

www.Volunteermatch.com

Local Ideas

Senior Homes

Hospitals

Daycares

Non-profits

Pet Shelters

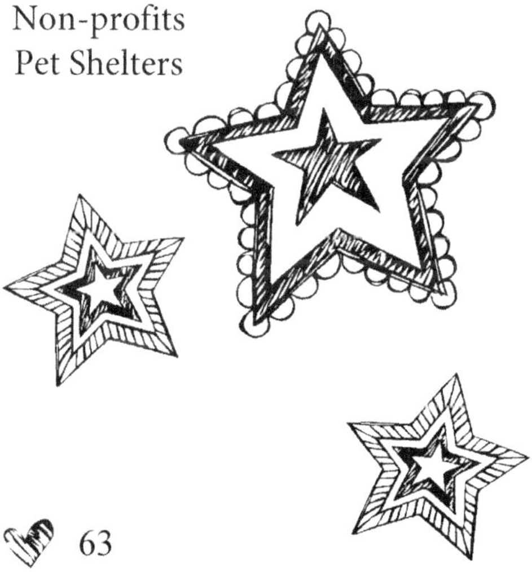

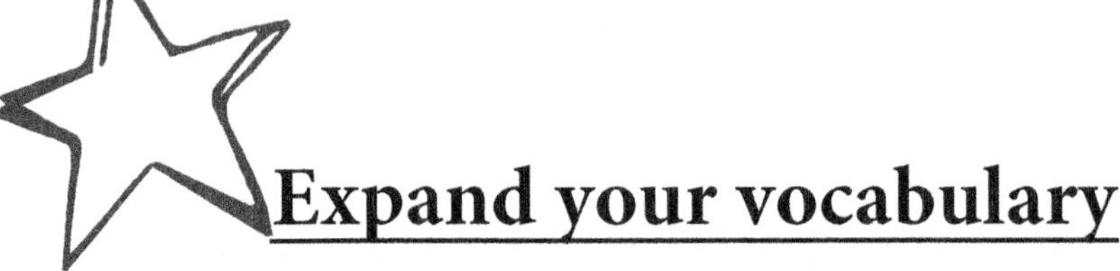

Expand your vocabulary

"Thot" and “fleek" aren't words you can write in a college essay. Be able to express yourself without cursing and using slang. Here’s an activity:

Find synonyms for the words listed below

Angry:

Good:

Happy:

Important:

Nervous:

Motivates:

Smart:

Practice what you preach

Do you give your friends advice and tell them to leave certain boys alone? Do you tell them not to hang out late and have sex all the time? If so, I hope you are taking your own advice. I knew I would be a therapist because I was always advising someone and then one day I looked at my life and realized I was not practicing what I preached. Shame on me.

TOP 5 VALUES

1.

2.

3.

4.

5.

Learn from your mistakes

Let's not continue to make the same bad decisions. I had to learn the hard way my sophomore year in high school. I totally flunked my second quarter in high school, (technically, I had one D amidst the F's) and I continued to cut school. Because of this my GPA went from a 3.67 to a 0.86. Then I had to live with my father in Pennsylvania and only stayed there two weeks before I was back in New Jersey. Once I got back, I still did not make the right decisions. I continued to make the same mistakes, well choices. At this point I knew exactly what the result would be. Let me clarify the difference between a mistake and a choice in my opinion. A mistake is something that you do one time without prior knowledge of the result or consequence. A choice is when you are aware of the consequence or the perceived result. Here's a shorter version: After the first time, IT IS NOT A MISTAKE. Ultimately, I knew the result was not what I wanted for myself.

Pat yourself on the back

I *NEVER* gave myself credit for the positivity I was exhibiting. Instead, I harped on the horrible things going on. So stop right now & pat yourself on the back. You're doing just fine!

Start a business

Indulge yourself in a business venture because it will motivate you to be a leader. We don't think enough about financial freedom and independence as teens. Learn to depend on yourself and your abilities. I was never sure if my mother was going to be talking to me, let alone give me spending money, so I did hair to make money.

Connect with your family

It is important to connect with your family because they are your first friends. They are the people that are innately connected to you and probably know the struggles you are experiencing. I did not connect with my family unless I had to and most of the time it was not genuine.

Fill in your family tree

The thrill isn't worth it

In college I became a thief. There was an adrenaline rush that come with shoplifting along with looking fly. While this happened in college, I know teens that do this. I shoplifted for about 5 months before I initially got caught. The loss prevention person thought I was attractive so he let me go with a warning. With that warning, I had to go pay for the items I tried to steal. You would laugh so loudly if you knew what I attempted to steal. I stopped shoplifting for a while, and then I started again because I missed the rush. It was to a point that I did not see the need to pay for certain things. Correction, I did not see the need to pay for most things. Money was to be spent on things I could not steal, like food. I even planned how to lift certain items if I did not get it the first time I saw it. Fast forward, I got caught a second time and the cops DID NOT care about my looks. I was arrested and taken to jail. I had a legit mugshot. Being in a cell by myself until the judge could see me, was an eye opener. I was let go and put on probation since it was my first offense.

I thought my name was Diamond

In high school I was so depressed and I wanted to escape my reality. I met this girl and we exchanged our teen struggles. I told her how I wanted to run away, but of course I didn't have money. She then talked to me about becoming a stripper. Since my bra size was a 36 C/D cup, I thought I could do it and would look old enough. I began to prep for this opportunity. I dyed my hair and started to mentally prepare myself for my new life. We talked again and she said we would travel around the world doing private parties which paid more money. It was with that conversation that I said "Oh HELL NO!" I knew it would be more than stripping and I was not ready for more trauma. God covered me that day because I was about to vanish.

Abuse is still abuse even when it's a family member

Many think you should not tell on a family member if they harm you. Most people will ignore the pain all together. Do not do this! Your experience is real and needs to be processed appropriately. I was 26 years old when I told my close friend, about things I endured as a kid. That was the first time I even said it out loud. Honestly, I am not sure how life would be different if I told when I was younger. I do know I thought it was "fine" and I do not want you to think the same. Family, friend or stranger, you should not be comfortable with any variation of abuse.

<u>Stop riding unless it's a bike</u>

If your dude goes to jail, what should you do?

~~STAY~~

MOVE ON

As a teenager there is no reason to be confined in that way. You will waste time in your life while you riding for him. Has it even occurred to you that you are worth more than someone that committed a crime or multiple crimes?

20-year-old and a 15-year-old

These ages mean something and before we truly begin, the biggest difference is statutory rape. ICYMI, most states define statutory rape as a 3 to 4-year age difference. Statutory rape is defined as sexual intercourse with minors. In most states, the age of consent is 16 years old and some states it is 18 years old. This means, until this age, you cannot consent for sex. I was 15 years old and I dated a guy that would end up taking my virginity. He was 20 years old and that makes a 5-year difference. I was not even ready to have sex; I just did it because I was rejected by the guy my age. Do not think that you need to do anything you are not 100% comfortable doing.

To ask or not to ask

Always ask questions. Through my various encounters I wish I would have asked certain questions for my own understanding. As teens, you often want to feel like an adult by making your own choices. You often think you know everything as well. Truth is, you do not. I spoke at my former high school and we were talking about sex. I decided to discuss menstrual cycles as a student prompted me. A freshman told me she did not understand what her menstrual cycle was for.

Tell me what you know about your cycle below

____

____

____

____

____

I am going to tell you what I told that group of freshman girls. "Every month your body is preparing for a baby and when it is unsuccessful you have your period. Yes! Every single month you could get pregnant unless you are already pregnant."

Green with envy

I was so jealous of my friends growing up as a teen. I was sure no one felt like I did and they appeared to have better family relationships. While this is easier said than done, don't be envious. Everyone has struggles; you just don't see them. Don't wish you were someone else or had what others have. Instead, think of how your trials will help you or others. Every struggle I endured led me here, to helping teens. This is something I am very proud of.

Love yourself

Do you know your values and morals? Do you have an internal compass to help guide you? Are you able to say no to things without feeling guilty if you do not like it? If you answered no to any of these questions, please take some time to get to know yourself. I had no idea who I was and I did not stand for anything. I was so depressed; I did anything that I thought would keep my mind off my sorrow. If I loved myself, I would not have done so many harmful things. In addition, a boy can't truly love you if you don't love yourself. Boys feed off your energy and only do what you allow.

LOVE YOURSELF

INFINITELY

Dear teen girl,

You are probably dealing with so many things in your life and I know you are confused with the decisions you are faced with. I've been there and that is why I decided to write this book. My troubles became my strength. I have learned that every mistake is a chance to grow and surpass any negative encounter endured. Do not give up on yourself! As the tears fall down my face, I hope this book helps you think differently about the struggles you are experiencing and how you can manage them. Although I do not know you personally, we share a bond that cannot be broken. I share your journey and I am here to encourage you to stay strong, as this phase will pass.

With Love,

Words to know

A

AIDS: AIDS stands for acquired immunodeficiency syndrome. AIDS is the final stage of HIV infection, and not everyone who has HIV advances to this stage. AIDS is the stage of infection that occurs when your immune system is badly damaged and you become vulnerable to *opportunistic infections.* a variable retrovirus that invades and inactivates helper T cells of the immune system and is a cause of AIDS and AIDS-related complex: variants were identified in several laboratories and independently named lymphadenopathy-associated virus (LAV) human T-cell lymphotropic virus type 3 (HTLV-3) and AIDS-related virus (ARV) the name human immunodeficiency virus (HIV) being subsequently proposed by an international taxonomy committee.

Anxiety: a feeling of worry, nervousness, or unease, typically about an imminent event or something with an uncertain outcome.

Anger: is an emotion characterized by antagonism toward someone or something you feel has deliberately done you wrong.

Attention: notice taken of someone or something; the regarding of someone or something as interesting or important.

B

Bullying: Use superior strength or influence to intimidate (someone), typically to force him or her to do what one wants.

C

Compassion: Sympathetic pity and concern for the sufferings or misfortunes of others.

Chlamydia: Is a common STD that can infect both men and women. It can cause serious, permanent damage to a woman's reproductive system, making it difficult or impossible for her to get pregnant later on. Chlamydia can also cause a potentially fatal ectopic pregnancy (pregnancy that occurs outside the womb).

Cervix: The narrow neck-like passage forming the lower end of the uterus.

Cyber bullying: Is when a child, preteen or teen is tormented, threatened, harassed, humiliated, embarrassed or otherwise targeted by another individual using the Internet, interactive and digital technologies including mobile phones.

D

Depression: Is a serious medical problem that causes a persistent feeling of sadness and loss of interest in activities. It affects how your teen thinks, feels and behaves, and it can cause emotional, functional and physical problems.

Determination: Firmness of purpose; resoluteness.

E

Eclectic: Deriving ideas, style, or taste from a broad and diverse range of sources.

Emotional Abuse: Is a form of abuse characterized by a person subjecting or exposing another to behavior that may result in psychological trauma, including anxiety, chronic depression, or post-traumatic stress disorder.

F

Fallopian tubes: Either of a pair of tubes along which eggs travel from the ovaries to the uterus.

G

Gonorrhea: A venereal disease involving inflammatory discharge from the urethra or vagina.

Genital warts- A small growth occurring in the anal or genital areas, caused by a virus that is spread especially by sexual contact.

H

HIV: HIV stands for human immunodeficiency virus. If left untreated, HIV can lead to the disease AIDS (acquired immunodeficiency syndrome).

HPV: HPV is the most common sexually transmitted infection (STI). HPV is a different virus than HIV and HSV (herpes). HPV is so common that nearly all sexually active men and women get it at some point in their lives. There are many different types of HPV. Some types can cause health problems including genital warts and cancers. There are vaccines that can stop these health problems from happening. Girls ages 11 or 12 years should get vaccinated.

Herpes: A virus causing contagious sores, most often around the mouth or on the genitals. Genital herpes is an STD caused by two types of viruses. The viruses are called herpes simplex type 1 and herpes simplex type 2.

I

Identity: In psychology, sociology, and anthropology, identity is a person's conception and expression of their own (self-identity) and others' individuality or group affiliations (such as national identity and cultural identity).

J K L

Love: An intense feeling of deep affection; a great interest and pleasure in something.

M N

Menstrual cycle: The monthly cycle of changes in the ovaries and the lining of the uterus (endometrium), starting with the preparation of an egg for fertilization. When the follicle of the prepared egg in the ovary breaks, it is released for fertilization and ovulation occurs. Unless pregnancy occurs, the cycle ends with the shedding of part of the endometrium, which is menstruation. Although it is actually the end of the physical cycle, the first day of menstrual bleeding is designated as "day 1" of the menstrual cycle in medical parlance.

O

Ovary: A female reproductive organ in which ova or eggs are produced, present in humans and other vertebrates as a pair.

P

Pregnancy: The state of carrying a developing embryo or fetus within the female body. This condition can be indicated by positive results on an over-the-counter urine test, and confirmed through a blood test, ultrasound, detection of fetal heartbeat, or an X-ray. Pregnancy lasts for about nine months, measured from the date of the woman's last menstrual period. It is conventionally divided into three trimesters, each roughly three months long.

Q R

Reproductive system: Is designed to carry out several functions. It produces the female egg cells necessary for reproduction, called the ova or oocytes. The system is designed to transport the ova to the site of fertilization. Conception, the fertilization of an egg by a sperm, normally occurs in the fallopian tubes. The next step for the fertilized egg is to implant into the walls of the uterus, beginning the initial stages of pregnancy. If fertilization and/or implantation does not take place, the system is designed to menstruate (the monthly shedding of the uterine lining). In addition, the female reproductive system produces female sex hormones that maintain the reproductive cycle.

S

STI: An infection transmitted through sexual contact, caused by bacteria, viruses, or parasites.

STD: Are generally acquired by sexual contact. The organisms that cause sexually transmitted diseases may pass from person to person in blood, semen, or vaginal and other bodily fluids.

Suicidal ideation: Thoughts about how to kill oneself, which can range from a detailed plan to a fleeting consideration and does not include the final act of killing oneself.

T

Trauma: Is an emotional response to a terrible event like an accident, rape or natural disaster. Immediately after the event, shock and denial are typical. Longer term reactions include unpredictable emotions, flashbacks, strained relationships and even physical symptoms like headaches or nausea. While these feelings are normal, some people have difficulty moving on with their lives

U V W X Y Z

Urinary tract infection: Is an infection in any part of your urinary system — your kidneys, ureters, bladder and urethra. Most infections involve the lower urinary tract — the bladder and the urethra.

Diary

Goals for 2016

Made in the USA
Monee, IL
28 June 2020

35004340R10066